Learning About Heat, Light, and Sound

Printed in China

ISBN 978-0-15-362220-5

ISBN 0-15-362220-2

9 10 0940 16 15 14 13

4500450571

Harcourt
SCHOOL PUBLISHERS

Visit *The Learning Site!*
www.harcourtschool.com

Learning About Heat, Light, and Sound

Requests for permission to make copies of any part of the work should be addressed to School Permissions and Copyrights, Harcourt, Inc., 6277 Sea Harbor Drive, Orlando, Florida 32887-6777. Fax: 407-345-2418.

Printed in China

ISBN 978-0-15-362220-5

ISBN 0-15-362220-2

9 10 0940 16 15 14 13

4500450571

Harcourt
SCHOOL PUBLISHERS

Visit *The Learning Site!*
www.harcourtschool.com

A raindrop can act like a prism. Sunlight refracted in a raindrop can separate into many colors.

Sunlight is really a mixture of colors. If you hold a prism to the sunlight, you will see different colors on the other side. This is because the light bends when it goes through the prism. When the sunlight bends, light is separated into its different colors.

You can use a prism and different colored paper to see how light can be absorbed or reflected on items differently. You will see all the colors on a sheet of white paper. On red paper, some colors can't be seen. This is because the red paper absorbs light of certain colors. The color of an object depends on its absorption or reflection of light.

Focus Skill **CAUSE AND EFFECT** **Why do you see many colors when sunlight passes through a prism?**

Heat moves by conduction from the fire to the pan. Conduction helps to cook this delicious fish!

Heat can move between objects that are touching each other. This type of heat movement is called **conduction**.

Some food cooks by conduction. When you put a frying pan on the stove burner and turn it on, the pan gets hot. When you put food in the hot pan, the food gets hot and cooks. When you eat the food, you can feel how warm it is.

The food cooks because of conduction. Heat moved from the hot pan to the food it was touching.

Focus Skill **MAIN IDEA AND DETAILS** **Why does a cold object that is touching a hot object become warm?**

Learning About Heat, Light, and Sound

Printed in China

ISBN 978-0-15-362220-5

ISBN 0-15-362220-2

9 10 0940 16 15 14 13

4500450571

Harcourt
SCHOOL PUBLISHERS

Visit *The Learning Site!*
www.harcourtschool.com

Heat Moves

Thermal energy is a form of energy that moves between objects of different temperatures. When you sit near a fireplace that is burning wood, you get warm. The fire is hotter than you, so the heat moves toward you.

Fast Fact

Many athletes who practice outdoors wear light-colored clothes. That's because dark colors get warm faster than light colors. Wearing light colors outdoors helps athletes stay cool!

The movement of thermal energy is called **heat**. The wood burning in the fireplace gives off heat. Because the fire is hotter than your body, the heat energy moves from the fire to your body.

Heat moves from this fireplace to whoever is sitting near it. Thermal energy can keep you warm.

Heat can move between objects that are touching each other. This type of heat movement is called **conduction**.

Some food cooks by conduction. When you put a frying pan on the stove burner and turn it on, the pan gets hot. When you put food in the hot pan, the food gets hot and cooks. When you eat the food, you can feel how warm it is.

The food cooks because of conduction. Heat moved from the hot pan to the food it was touching.

Focus Skill **MAIN IDEA AND DETAILS** **Why does a cold object that is touching a hot object become warm?**

Light Moves

Light travels in a straight line. It continues to travel in the same straight line until it strikes an object.

What happens when light bumps into an object? Some of the light bounces off the object. This is called **reflection**. Every object that you can see is visible because of reflection. If an object is very smooth or shiny, it reflects most of the light.

This lake is smooth enough to make a reflection of the forest.

Sometimes light bends. The bending of light as it moves from one material to another is called **refraction**.

If you put part of your finger in water, you can see the difference between reflection and refraction. Your finger above the water looks the same as you always see it. Light bounces off it straight to your eyes.

But the part of your finger below the water might seem bent or even disconnected from the rest of your finger! That's because light bends when it goes through the water.

When light moves from air to the water, it bends. The straw looks bent below the surface of the water.

You see the part of your finger above the water by reflection. You see the part of your finger below the water by refraction. The bending light makes it look like your finger is not connected below the water.

Focus Skill **SEQUENCE** **What happens to light after it hits water?**

You and Your Shadow

Suppose an object, like a building, stands in the path of sunlight. As a result, you might see its shadow. A **shadow** is the dark area that forms when an object blocks or absorbs the path of light.

Shadows form when any kind of light is blocked, not just light from the sun. If you hold your hand between a lamp and the wall, you might see your hand's shadow on the wall. That is because your hand has blocked, or absorbed, the light from the lamp.

Fast Fact

During a solar eclipse, the moon passes between the sun and the Earth. On Earth, the sky darkens. The moon casts a shadow on Earth!

You can use your hands or other objects to make shadows that are fun!

Shadows made from the sun change during the day. Both the position and the shape of shadows change.

Shadows are longer when the sun is low in the sky than when the sun is high in the sky. This means that shadows are longer in the early morning and late afternoon, than at midday.

As the sun appears to move across the sky, the direction of shadows change. In the morning when the sun is on one side of a building, its shadow might appear in one position. In the late afternoon when the sun is on the other side of the same building, the building's shadow appears somewhere else!

Focus Skill **SEQUENCE How do shadows change—from early morning, to midday, to late afternoon?**

At the end of the day, shadows are longer. That's because the sun is lower in the sky.

Colors

Light can be reflected, refracted, and absorbed. When light is **absorbed**, it is taken in by the object. Objects that are dull or dark absorb most of the light that hits them. Cement, bricks, and rocks absorb most of the light that strikes them.

Different objects react differently to light. People, wooden chairs, and mirrors are all objects that do not let any light pass through them. Sheer curtains on a window let some light pass through them. A clear glass bowl, a drinking glass, or a window lets almost all light pass through it.

Frosted light bulbs let some light pass through them, but you can't see what's inside.

Fast Fact

Why is the sky blue? Water drops in the air absorb light and reflect it as the color blue. Water drops in clouds reflect the light as white.

A raindrop can act like a prism. Sunlight refracted in a raindrop can separate into many colors.

Sunlight is really a mixture of colors. If you hold a prism to the sunlight, you will see different colors on the other side. This is because the light bends when it goes through the prism. When the sunlight bends, light is separated into its different colors.

You can use a prism and different colored paper to see how light can be absorbed or reflected on items differently. You will see all the colors on a sheet of white paper. On red paper, some colors can't be seen. This is because the red paper absorbs light of certain colors. The color of an object depends on its absorption or reflection of light.

Focus Skill **CAUSE AND EFFECT** **Why do you see many colors when sunlight passes through a prism?**

Sound

Have you ever watched someone play a guitar? The guitar player plucks the strings, making them move back and forth. These back-and-forth movements are **vibrations**. They make the air around the strings vibrate. People hear the air's vibration as sound.

There are many ways to make sound. Blowing, plucking, and tapping are ways to make sound with a musical instrument. Each makes the air vibrate in a different way.

Tapping a drum makes the air vibrate in a certain way. Dropping a pencil makes the air around it vibrate in a different way. Even the loud engine of a truck makes the air around it vibrate in a certain way.

Playing each of these drums or cymbals makes the air vibrate in a special way.

The air vibrating around this tea kettle makes a "whistling" sound.

Different objects make different sounds. This is because they vibrate the air around them in a different way.

You hear the sounds because the vibrations in the air travel to your ears. The vibrating air makes your eardrums vibrate, and you hear sound.

A car's horn, a door slamming, a trumpet—all of these things make the air vibrate a certain way. Then the vibrating air comes to you and hits your eardrums. That makes your eardrum vibrate a certain way and you hear the sound. Vibrations are important to making sound and to hearing sound.

Focus Skill **MAIN IDEA AND DETAILS** **Does a lion's growl cause the air outside of its throat to vibrate? How can you tell?**

Turn Up the Volume

Have you ever been near a bird when it whistled? Have you ever been near a cymbal when someone hit it? Both the bird and the cymbal make a sound. But one sound is louder than the other. **Loudness** is how much energy a sound has.

Suppose you tap a drum without using much force. It will not sound very loud. What happens if you bang the drum as hard as you can? When you hit the drum hard, the vibrations have more energy. The sound is louder.

The siren on this fire truck needs to be loud so people can hear it and move out of the way.

Higher volume means more sound energy.

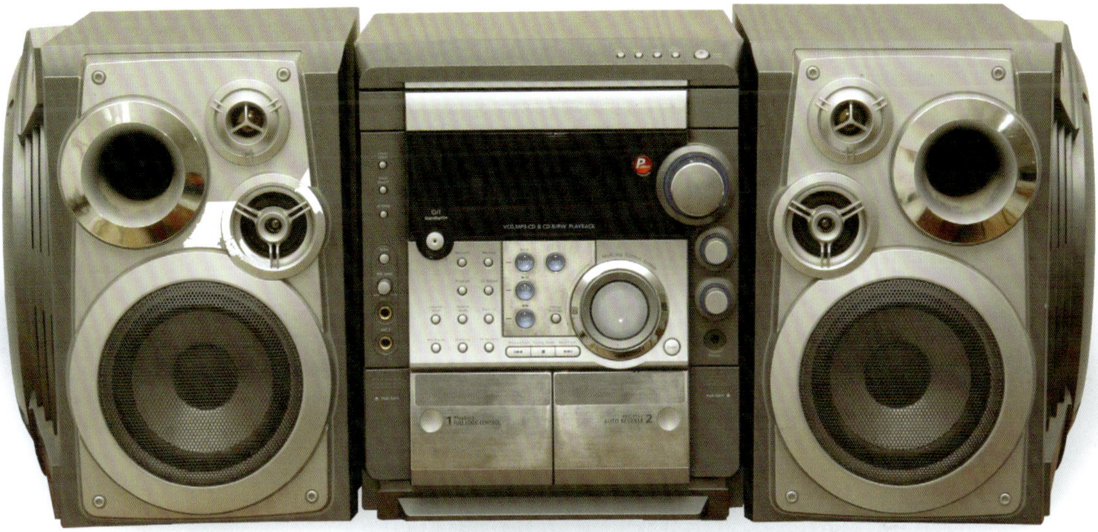

You don't need to be a scientist to figure out if a sound has much energy. You can tell if a sound has a lot of energy by listening to it. Loud sounds have more energy that quiet sounds.

You can measure how much energy is in a sound. **Volume** measures the loudness of sound.

Televisions, CD players, and stereos all have a volume control. This lets you change how loud the sound will be.

Focus Skill **MAIN IDEA AND DETAILS** **If one sound is louder than another, what does that tell you about the sound energy in each one?**

High and Low Sounds

You can make many different sounds when you play a musical instrument. If you strike a key at one end of a piano keyboard, you make a high sound. If you strike a key at the other end, you make a low sound. **Pitch** tells us if a sound is high or low. Guitars, trumpets, saxophones, harmonicas—most musical instruments—make both high and low sounds.

You can change pitch by changes in length, thickness, and tension. Playing a thicker guitar string gives a lower sound than a thinner string. Striking a shorter piano string gives a higher sound than striking a longer string.

Focus Skill **MAIN IDEA AND DETAILS What does the pitch of the music from a piano tell us about sound?**

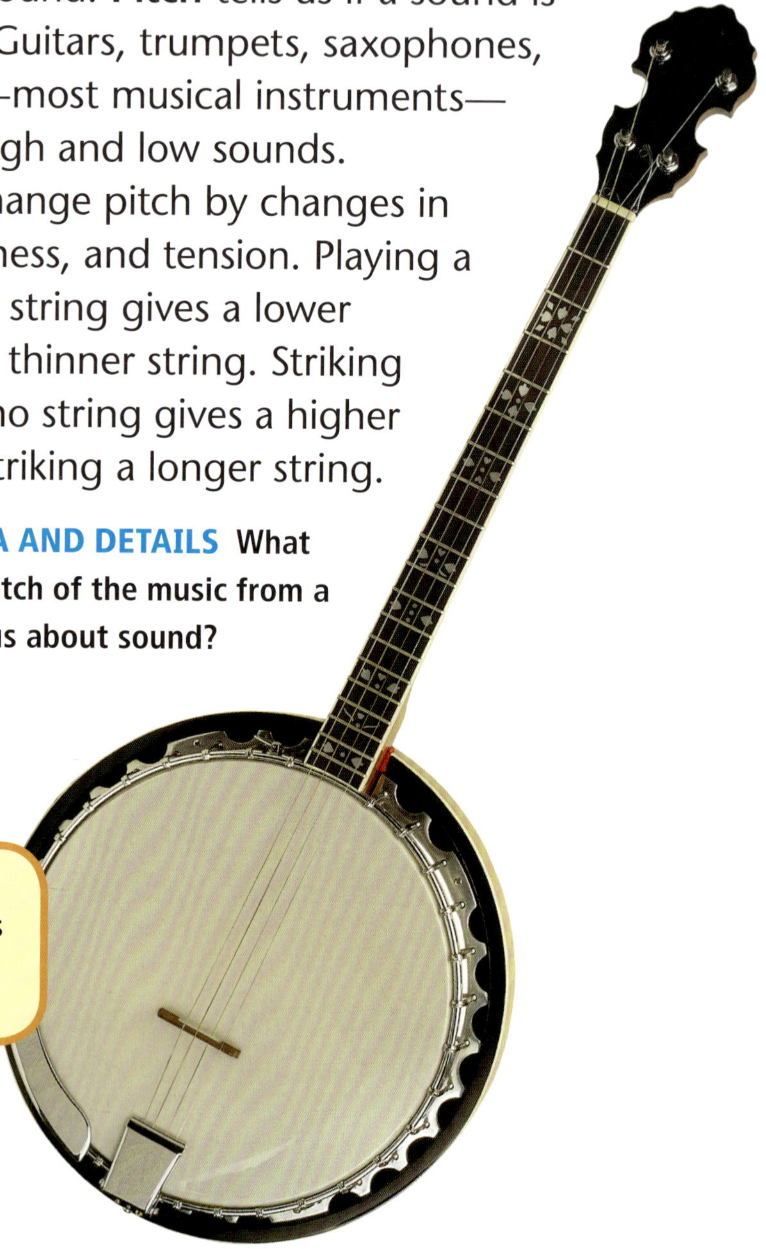

A banjo player can make music that has either a high- or a low-pitched sound.

Light and sound energy travel all over this concert hall.

Summary

The world is full of energy! Heat is the movement of thermal energy. Conduction moves the heat through objects. Light travels through air in a straight line, unless it hits an object. Then, it is reflected, refracted, or absorbed. Light also makes shadows when it hits an object. Sound is made from vibrations. Volume tells you how loud a sound is. Pitch tells you how high or low a sound is.

Fast Fact

Adult women's voices usually have a higher pitch than men's voices. That's because most women have thinner vocal cords than men. The cords vibrate more quickly, making higher-pitched sounds!

Glossary

absorbed (ab•SAWRBD) Taken in by an object (6, 8, 9, 15)

conduction (kuhn•DUK•shuhn) The movement of heat between objects that are touching each other (3, 15)

heat (HEET) The movement of thermal energy from hotter to cooler objects (2, 3, 15)

loudness (LOUD•nuhs) How much energy a sound has (13, 15)

pitch (PICH) How high or low a sound is (14, 15)

reflection (rih•FLEK•shuhn) The bouncing of light off an object (4, 5, 9, 15)

refraction (rih•FRAK•shuhn) The bending of light as it moves from one material to another (5, 15)

shadow (SHAD•oh) A dark area that forms when an object blocks the path of light (6, 7, 15)

thermal energy (THER•muhl EN•er•jee) The form of energy that moves particles of matter (2, 15)

vibrations (vy•BRAY•shuhnz) A series of back-and-forth movements (10, 11, 12, 15)

volume (VAHL•yoom) The loudness of a sound (12, 13, 15)